SILLY JOKES FOR KIDS
JOKE BOOK WITH CARTOONS

© 2019 by PlayHouse Publishing

All rights reserved. No part of this publication may be reproduced, stored in a retrieval system, or transmitted in any form or by any means – for example, electronic, photocopy, and recording – without the prior written permission of the publisher. The only exception is brief quotations in printed reviews.

Jokes and Cartoons

Question

What do you call a sleeping bull?

Answer

A bulldozer!

Question

What did the fisherman say to the magician?

Answer

Pick a cod, any cod!

Joke Book – Silly Jokes for Silly Kids

Question

What do you call cheese that does not belong to you?

Answer

Nach-o cheese!

Question

Why was the broom late?

Answer

It over swept!

Jokes and Cartoons

Question

Why do golfers wear two pairs of pants?

Answer

In case they get a hole in one!

Question

What did the calculator say to the math student?

Answer

You can count on me!

Joke Book – Silly Jokes for Silly Kids

Question

Why do dragons sleep during the day?

Answer

So they can fight knights!

Question

What did the blanket say to the bed?

Answer

Don't worry, I've got you covered!

Jokes and Cartoons

Question

What did the buffalo say to his kid when he dropped him off at school?

Answer

Bison!

Question

What did the tree say to the wind?

Answer

Leaf me alone!

Joke Book – Silly Jokes for Silly Kids

Question

What do you call a pig that has mastered karate?

Answer

A pork chop!

Question

What did one wall say to the other wall?

Answer

I'll meet you at the corner!

Jokes and Cartoons

Question

What kind of shoes do most spies wear?

Answer

Sneak-ers!

Question

Why did the drum want to take a nap?

Answer

It was beat!

Joke Book – Silly Jokes for Silly Kids

Question

What type of music do planets listen to?

Answer

Nep-tunes!

Question

What does a penny say to another penny?

Answer

We make cents!

Question

Why did the banana go to the hospital?

Answer

The banana wasn't peeling very well!

Question

What followed the dinosaur?

Answer

It's tail!

Question

What do you find in an empty nose?

Answer

Fingerprints!

Joke Book – Silly Jokes for Silly Kids

Question

What do you call a cow on a trampoline?

Answer

A milk shake!

Question

Why did the man run around his bed?

Answer

Because he was trying to catch up on his sleep!

Question

What do you call a Barbie doll that gets cooked?

Answer

A Barbie que!

Question

What do you get if you cross a cat with a parrot?

Answer

A carrot!

Question

What do you call a dentist in the army?

Answer

A drill sergeant!

Joke Book – Silly Jokes for Silly Kids

Question

What did the teacher say to the lightbulb?

Answer

Well, aren't you bright!

Question

Why don't people use dull pencils?

Answer

What's the point?

Question

Did you hear about the kidnapping at the school?

Answer

Its ok, he woke up!

Jokes and Cartoons

Question

When do doctors get mad?

Answer

When they run out of patients!

Question

What do you get when you cross a snake with a pie?

Answer

A pie-thon!

Joke Book – Silly Jokes for Silly Kids

Question

What's the most musical part of the chicken?

Answer

The drumstick!

Question

Why did the teacher wear sunglasses inside?

Answer

Her students were so bright!

Question

Why was the nose so tired?

Answer

Because it had been running all day!

Question

What do you get when you cross a caterpillar and a parrot?

Answer

A walkie talkie!

Question

What do you get when you cross a fish with an elephant?

Answer

Swimming trunks!

Joke Book – Silly Jokes for Silly Kids

Question

What do you get when you cross a bank with a skunk?

Answer

Dollars and scents!

Question

What do you get when you cross a wolf and an egg?

Answer

A very hairy omelette!

Question

What do you get if you cross a cow and a camel?

Answer

Lumpy milkshakes!

Question

Why shouldn't you tell an egg a joke?

Answer

Because it might crack up!

Question

What did one eye say to the other eye?

Answer

Don't look now, but something between us smells!

Joke Book – Silly Jokes for Silly Kids

Question

Why do some people stare at bottles of orange juice?

Answer

Because the bottles say concentrate!

Question

How do prisoners call each other?

Answer

Cell phones!

Question

Why is 6 afraid of 7?

Answer

Because 7 8 9!

Jokes and Cartoons

Question

What kind of key opens a banana?

Answer

A monkey!

Question

What do elves learn in school?

Answer

The elf-abet!

Joke Book – Silly Jokes for Silly Kids

Question

What's the worst thing about throwing a party in space?

Answer

You have to planet!

Question

Why did the scientist take out his doorbell?

Answer

He wanted to win the no-bell prize!

Question

What did one firefly say to the other?

Answer

You glow girl!

Jokes and Cartoons

Question

What time is it if an elephant sits on the fence?

Answer

Time to fix the fence!

Question

What sound do porcupines make when they hug?

Answer

Ouch!

Joke Book – Silly Jokes for Silly Kids

Question

When does a computer go to a doctor?

Answer

When

It has a virus!

Question

What did the grape do when it got stepped on?

Answer

It let out a little wine!

Question

Why should you take a pencil to bed?

Answer

To draw the curtains!

Jokes and Cartoons

Question

Why are pirates called pirates?

Answer

Cause they arrrrr!

Question

What did the flower say to the bike?

Answer

Petal!

Joke Book – Silly Jokes for Silly Kids

Question

What do you call a rabbit with fleas?

Answer

Bugs bunny!

Question

What did the nose say to the finger?

Answer

Stop picking on me!

Question

What kind of bed does a mermaid sleep in?

Answer

A water bed!

Question

What's a snake's favorite subject?

Answer

Hissss-tory!

Question

Where do pencils go on vacation?

Answer

Pencil-vania!

Joke Book – Silly Jokes for Silly Kids

Question

What did the judge say to the dentist?

Answer

Do you swear to pull the tooth, the whole tooth, and nothing but the tooth?

Question

Where do sheep go to get their hair cut?

Answer

The baaa-baaa shop!

Question

What do call it when you help a lemon that's in trouble?

Answer

Lemon-aid!

Jokes and Cartoons

Question

When's the best time to go to the dentist?

Answer

Tooth-hurty!

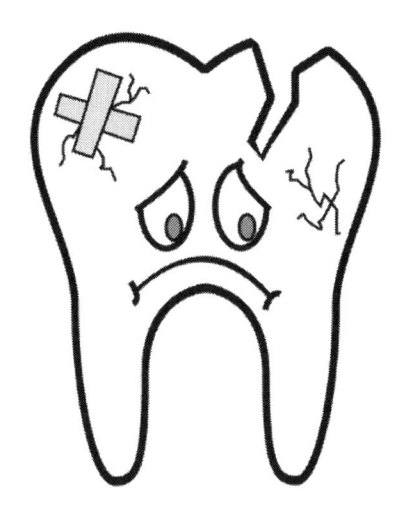

Question

What has four wheels and flies?

Answer

A garbage truck!

Joke Book – Silly Jokes for Silly Kids

Question

Why did the teenager take a ladder to school?

Answer

Because he thought it was a HIGH school!

Question

Which flower talks the most?

Answer

Tu-lips!

Question

What do you call a wannabe noodle?

Answer

An Im-pasta

Jokes and Cartoons

Question

Where do cows go for entertainment?

Answer

The mooooooo-vies!

Question

What kind of button can you not undo?

Answer

Your belly button!

Joke Book – Silly Jokes for Silly Kids

Question

Why did the boy eat his homework?

Answer

Because his teacher said it was a piece of cake!

Question

Why can you never trust atoms?

Answer

They make up everything!

Question

What did the triangle say to the circle?

Answer

You're pointless!

Jokes and Cartoons

Question

What animal needs to wear a wig?

Answer

A bald eagle!

Question

What did Bacon say to Tomato?

Answer

Lettuce get together!

Question

Why did the soccer player bring string to the game?

Answer

So he could tie the score!

Question

Who cleans the bottom of the ocean?

Answer

A Mer-Maid!

Question

Why won't the elephant use the computer?

Answer

They're afraid of the mouse!

Question

Why do bees have sticky hair?

Answer

Because they use honeycombs!

Question

What musical instrument is found in the bathroom?

Answer

A tuba toothpaste!

Question

What kind of snack do you have during a scary movie?

Answer

I scream!

Question

Why don't skeletons fight each other?

Answer

They don't have the guts!

Question

What is a robot's favorite snack?

Answer

Computer chips!

Question

How do you make a tissue dance?

Answer

Put a little boogey in it!

Question

What do you get from a pampered cow?

Answer

Spoiled milk!

Joke Book – Silly Jokes for Silly Kids

Question

What do you call an alligator in a vest?

Answer

An investigator!

Question

What goes up and down but does not move?

Answer

Stairs!

Question

What do you get when you cross fish and an elephant?

Answer

Swimming trunks!

Question

What did the judge say when the skunk walked in the court room?

Answer

Odor in the court!

Question

Why did the math book look so sad?

Answer

Because it had so many problems!

Question

What do you get when you cross a snowman with a shark?

Answer

Frostbite!

Question

What do you get when you cross a frog with a rabbit?

Answer

A bunny ribbit!

Question

What do you get when you cross a chicken and a Chihuahua?

Answer

Pooched eggs!

Jokes and Cartoons

Question

Why did the tomato become red?

Answer

It saw the salad dressing!

Question

How many tickles does it take to make an octopus laugh?

Answer

Ten-tickles!

Joke Book – Silly Jokes for Silly Kids

Question

What did one toilet say to the other?

Answer

You look a bit flushed!

Question

Why do bicycles fall over?

Answer

Because they are two-tired!

Question

Which hand is it better to write with?

Answer

Neither, it's best to write with a pen!

Jokes and Cartoons

Question

How do rabbits travel?

Answer

By hare plane!

Question

What did one potato chip say to the other?

Answer

Shall we go for a dip?

Joke Book – Silly Jokes for Silly Kids

Question

What do you call a man who does not have all his fingers on one hand?

Answer

You have fingers on both hands!

Question

What is the best cure for dandruff?

Answer

Baldness!

Question

What did the chewing gum say to the shoe?

Answer

I am stuck on you!

Jokes and Cartoons

Question

What do you get when you cross a lizard and a baby?

Answer

A creepy crawler!

Question

What do you get when you cross a cheetah & a hamburger?

Answer

Fast Food!

Question

Why kind of food can increase your eyesight?

Answer

Seafood!

Question

Why couldn't the pony sing himself a lullaby?

Answer

He was a little hoarse!

Question

What do you get when you cross a fish and drumsticks?

Answer

Fish sticks!

Jokes and Cartoons

Question

What did the paper say to the pencil?

Answer

Write on!

Question

What did baby corn say to his mama corn?

Answer

Where is popcorn?

Joke Book – Silly Jokes for Silly Kids

Question

What do you call a belt with a watch on it?

Answer

A waist of time!

Question

What did the traffic light say to the car?

Answer

Don't look, I'm changing!

Question

How do you find a Princess?

Answer

You follow the foot Prince!

Question

What do you call a deer with no eyes?

Answer

No-Eye Deer!

Question

Why did the boy throw the butter out the window?

Answer

To see a butterfly!

Question

What kind of dinosaur loves to sleep?

Answer

A stega-snore-us!

Question

Why do moon rocks taste better than earth rocks?

Answer

Because they're meteor!

Question

What do you call a funny mountain?

Answer

Hill-arious!

Question

Why do sea-gulls fly over the sea?

Answer

Because if they flew over the bay they would be bagels!

Question

Where do you learn to make a banana split?

Answer

Sundae school!

Joke Book – Silly Jokes for Silly Kids

Question

What do you call a bear with no socks on?

Answer

Bare-foot!

Question

What do you call two bananas?

Answer

Slippers!

Question

Where do hamburgers go to dance?

Answer

They go to the meat-ball!

Question

What do you get when you cross a fridge with a radio?

Answer

Cool Music!

Question

Why did the cookie go to the hospital?

Answer

He felt crummy!

Question

Where do snowmen keep their money?

Answer

In snow banks!

Question

What does a nosey pepper do?

Answer

Gets jalapeno business!

Question

How do you know when the moon has had a lot to eat?

Answer

When it's full!

Jokes and Cartoons

Question

When is it bad luck to be followed by a black cat?

Answer

When you're a mouse!

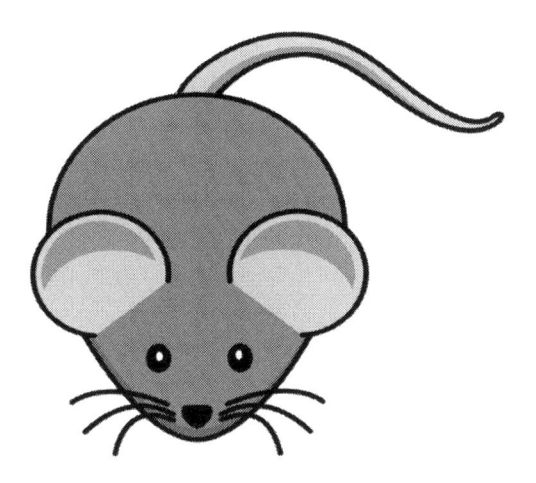

Question

Why did the hamburger go to the gym?

Answer

He wanted to beef up!

Joke Book – Silly Jokes for Silly Kids

Question

Why do you go to bed every night?

Answer

Because the bed won't come to you!

Question

What washes up on very small beaches?

Answer

Microwaves!

Question

Why are teddy bears never hungry?

Answer

They are always stuffed!

Question

What kind of crackers do firemen like in their soup?

Answer

Firecrackers!

Question

How does an ocean say hello?

Answer

It waves!

Joke Book – Silly Jokes for Silly Kids

Knock knock!

Who's there?

Isabell!

Isabell who?

Is a bell working?

Knock knock!

Who's there?

Annie!

Annie who?

Annie body home?

Joke Book – Silly Jokes for Silly Kids

Knock knock!

Who's there?

Harry!

Harry who?

Harry up, it's cold out here!

Knock knock!

Who's there?

Mikey!

Mikey who?

Mikey doesn't fit in the keyhole!

Knock knock!

Who's there?

Orange!

Orange who?

Orange you going to let me in?

Knock knock!

Who's there?

Who

Who, who?

Are you an owl?

Knock knock!

Who's there?

Ice Cream!

Ice Cream who?

Ice Cream if you don't let me in!

Knock knock!

Who's there?

Doughnut!

Doughnut Who?

Doughnut ask, it's a secret!

Knock Knock Jokes

Knock knock!

Who's there?

Wooden Shoe!

Wooden shoe who?

Wooden you like to hear another knock, knock joke?!

Knock knock!

Who's there?

Police!

Police who?

Police let us in, it's raining outside!

Knock knock!

Who's there?

Atch!

Atch who?

Bless you!

Knock knock!

Who's there?

Figs!

Figs who?

Figs the doorbell, it's broken!

Knock knock!

Who's there?

Yodel-lay-he!

Yodel-lay-he-who?

Yodel-lay-he-who, I didn't know you can yodel!

Knock knock!

Who's there?

Cash

Cash who?

No thanks, I prefer peanuts!

Knock knock!

Who's there?

Banana!

Banana who?

Knock knock!

Who's there?

Banana!

Banana who?

Knock knock!

Who's there?

Banana!

Banana who?

Knock knock!

Who's there?

Orange!

Orange who?

Orange you glad I didn't say banana!

Knock knock!

Who's there?

Olive!

Olive who?

Olive right next to you!

Knock knock!

Who's there?

Boo!

Boo who?

Don't cry, it's just me!

Joke Book – Silly Jokes for Silly Kids

Knock knock!

Who's there?

Doris!

Doris who?

Doris locked, that's why I knocked!

Knock knock!

Who's there?

Leaf?

Leaf who?

Leaf me alone!

Knock knock!

Who's there?

Canoe!

Canoe who?

Canoe come over and play!

Knock knock!

Who's there?

Justin!

Justin who?

Justin time for lunch!

Knock knock!

Who's there?

Jess!

Jess who?

Jess me and my shadow!

Knock knock!

Who's there?

Nanna!

Nanna who?

Nanna ya business!

Knock knock!

Who's there?

Spell!

Spell who?

W, H, O!

Knock knock!

Who's there?

Luke!

Luke who?

Luke through the keyhole and you'll see!

Knock knock!

Who's there?

Goat!

Goat who?

Goat to the door and see!

Knock knock!

Who's there?

Norma Lee!

Norma Lee who?

Norma Lee I don't go around knocking on doors!

Knock knock!

Who's there?

Cook!

Cook who?

Hey! Who are you calling cuckoo?

Knock knock!

Who's there?

Watson!

Watson who?

What's on tv tonight?

Knock knock!

Who's there?

Alex!

Alex who?

Alex-plain later!

Knock knock!

Who's there?

Car go!

Car go who?

Car go BEEP!

Knock knock!

Who's there?

Wanda!

Wanda who?

Wanda hang out with me right now?

Knock knock!

Who's there?

Irish.

Irish who?

Irish you a Merry Christmas!

Knock knock!

Who's there?

Ya!

Ya who?

I'm excited to see you too!

Knock knock!

Who's there?

Needle!

Needle who?

Needle little help getting in the door!

Knock knock!

Who's there?

Wendy!

Wendy who?

Wendy bell works again I won't have to knock anymore.

Knock knock!

Who's there?

Tank!

Tank who?

You're welcome!

Joke Book – Silly Jokes for Silly Kids

Question

What has hands but cannot clap?

Answer

A clock!

Question

What starts with the letter "t", is filled with "t" and ends in "t"?

Answer

A teapot!

Question

What gets wetter and wetter the more it dries?

Answer

A Towel!

Joke Book – Silly Jokes for Silly Kids

Question

Which weighs more, a pound of feathers or a pound of bricks?

Answer

Neither, they both weigh one pound!

Question

What's full of holes but still holds water?

Answer

A sponge!

Question

The more you take, the more you leave behind! What are they?

Answer

Footprints!

Silly Riddles

Question

What goes up when rain comes down?

Answer

An umbrella!

Question

What kind of tree can you carry in your hand?

Answer

A palm!

Question

How many months have 28 days?

Answer

All 12 months!

Joke Book – Silly Jokes for Silly Kids

Question

How can a man go 8 days without sleep?

Answer

He only sleeps at night.

Question

What can you catch but not throw?

Answer

A cold!

Question

If I drink, I die! If I eat, I am fine! What am I?

Answer

A fire!

Silly Riddles

Question

What belongs to you, but other people use it more than you?

Answer

Your name!

Question

What is more useful when it is broken?

Answer

An egg!

Question

What has a head, a tail, is brown, and has no legs?

Answer

A penny!

Joke Book – Silly Jokes for Silly Kids

Question

How can you leave a room with two legs and return with six legs?

Answer

Bring a chair back with you!

Question

I am white when I am dirty, and black when I am clean! What am I?

Answer

Blackboard!

Question

What word contains all of the twenty six letters?

Answer

Alphabet!

Question

What can you hold without ever touching or using your hands?

Answer

Your breath!

Question

Before Mt! Everest was discovered, what was the highest mountain in the world?

Answer

Mt! Everest! It just had not been discovered yet!

Question

What five-letter word becomes shorter when you add two letters to it?

Answer

Short!

Question

Bobby throws a ball and it comes back to him without being touched. How?

Answer

He throws it straight up!

Question

Mary's father has five daughters – Nana, Nene, Nini, Nono! What is the fifth daughter's name?

Answer

Mary!

Question

If an electric train is travelling south, which way is the smoke going?

Answer

There is no smoke; it is an electric train!

Silly Riddles

Question

You draw a line! Without touching it, how do you make the line longer?

Answer

You draw a shorter line next to it, and then it becomes the longer line!

Question

Which word in the dictionary is spelled incorrectly?

Answer

Incorrectly!

Question

I do not have wings, but I can fly! I don't have eyes, but I will cry! What am I?

Answer

A cloud!

Question

I am full of keys, but I cannot open any door! What am I?

Answer

A piano!

Question

You can break me easily without even touching me or seeing me! What am I?

Answer

A promise!

Question

The more you take away, the larger it becomes? What is it?

Answer

A hole!

Question

I am tall when I am young and I am short when I am old! What am I?

Answer

A candle!

Question

What has a thumb and four fingers but is not alive?

Answer

A glove!

Question

If you are running in a race and you pass the person in the second place, what place are you in?

Answer

Second place!

Joke Book – Silly Jokes for Silly Kids

Question

I lose my head every morning, but get it back at night! What Am I?

Answer

A pillow!

Question

I am a type of vehicle! I am spelled the same way forwards and backwards! What Am I?

Answer

Race car!

Question

A rooster laid an egg on top of the barn roof! Which way did it roll?

Answer

It didn't roll – roosters don't lay eggs!

Silly Riddles

Question

How much dirt is there in a hole 3 feet deep, 6ft long and 4ft wide?

Answer

None!

Question

What is at the end of a rainbow?

Answer

The letter "w".

Question

I make two people out of one! What am I?

Answer

A mirror!

Joke Book – Silly Jokes for Silly Kids

Question

What fruit has its seeds on the outside?

Answer

A strawberry!

Question

You answer me, but I never ask you a question! What am I?

Answer

A telephone!

Question

David's father has three sons: Snap, Crackle and……!! ?

Answer

David!

Question

What runs around the whole yard without moving?

Answer

A Fence!

Question

Which letter of the alphabet has the most water?

Answer

C!

Question

Why did the boy bury his flashlight?

Answer

Because the batteries died!

Question

What occurs once in a minute, twice in a moment, and never in one thousand years?

Answer

The letter M!

Question

What is so delicate that saying its name breaks it?

Answer

Silence!

Question

What invention lets you look right through a wall?

Answer

A window!

Question

How can a pants pocket be empty and still have something in it?

Answer

It can have a hole in it!

Question

People buy me to eat, but never eat me. What am I?

Answer

A plate!

Question

It has a neck but no head. What is it?

Answer

A bottle!

Joke Book – Silly Jokes for Silly Kids

Question

You can you serve it, but never eat it? What is it?

Answer

A tennis ball!

Question

What goes up and never comes down?

Answer

Your age!

Made in the USA
Middletown, DE
19 June 2019